MW00389003

1

PIANO
Adventures®

Challenging pieces with
changing moods and
changing hand positions

by Nancy and Randall Faber

THE BASIC PIANO METHOD

Production Coordinator: Jon Ophoff
Design and Illustration: Terpstra Design, San Francisco

FABER
PIANO ADVENTURES®

ISBN 978-1-61677-604-6

Table of Contents

("Gold Star" characteristics of each piece)
Color the star gold or put a star sticker for each piece you learn!

FF1604

I Love the Mountains

Traditional Words and Music
Arranged by Nancy Faber

Moderate swing (long-short pattern for 8th notes)

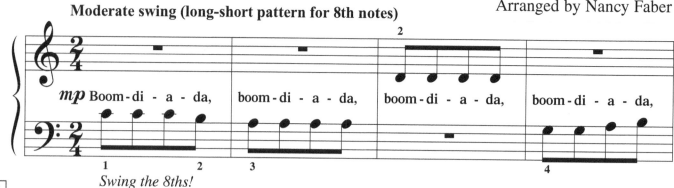

Swing the 8ths!

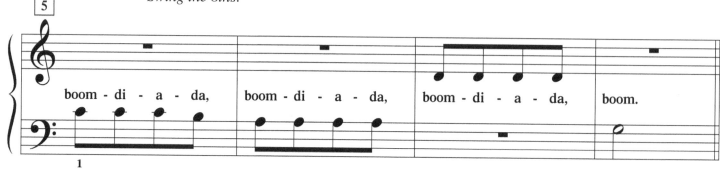

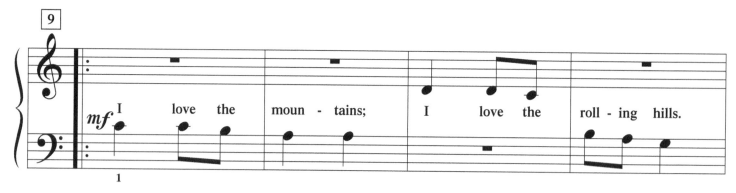

Teacher Duet: (Student plays 1 octave higher)

Repeat from measure 9.

FF1604

DISCOVERY What does $\frac{2}{4}$ mean? Write **1 2** above the beats for *measures 1–8.*

Five-Note Sonatina

Oscar Bolck
(1839–1888)
original form

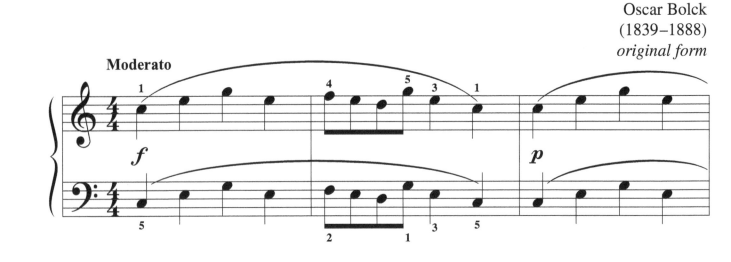

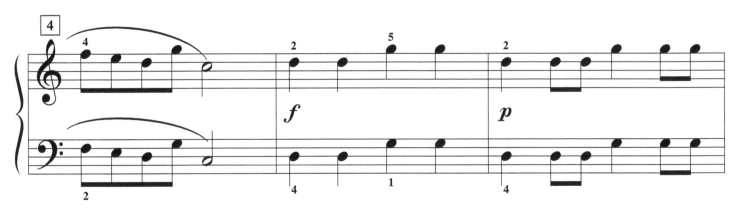

Teacher Duet: (Student plays 1 octave higher)

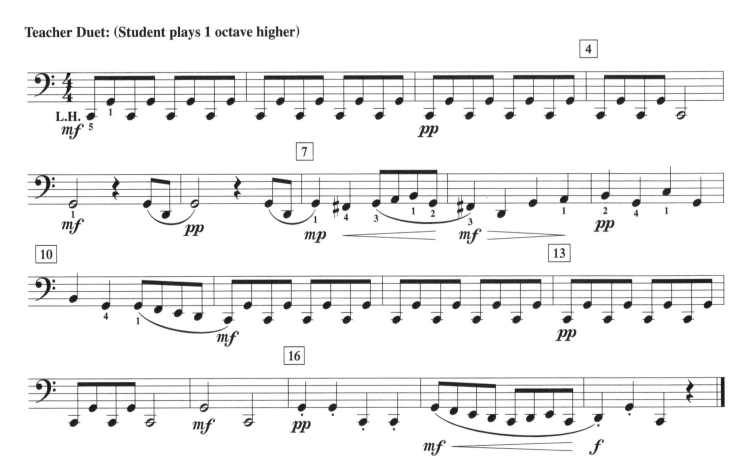

FF1604

DISCOVERY

parallel motion — moving in the *same* direction.
contrary motion — moving in the *opposite* direction.

Does *Five-Note Sonatina* use **parallel** motion or **contrary** motion?

There's Nothing Like a Circus

Words by Jennifer MacLean
Music by Nancy Faber

FF1604

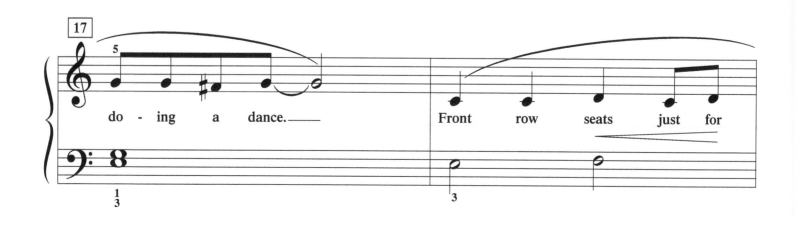

do - ing a dance._____ Front row seats just for

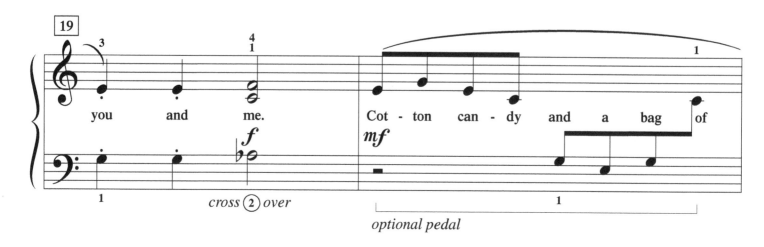

you and me. Cot - ton can - dy and a bag of

cross ②*over*

optional pedal

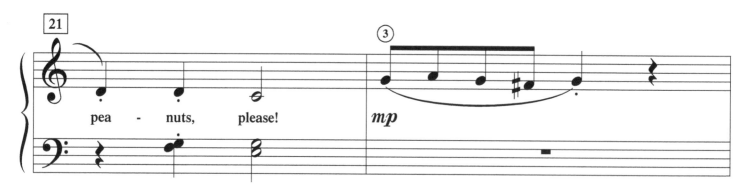

pea - nuts, please! *mp*

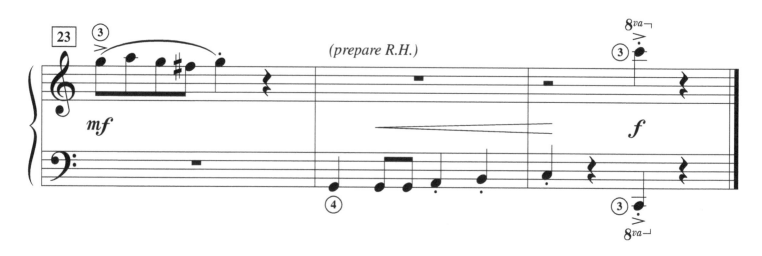

(prepare R.H.)

DISCOVERY   A **phrase** is a musical sentence. A phrase is shown with a slur, called a **phrase mark**.
Point out the first 3 phrases in this piece.

Little Ghost's Recital

Nancy Faber

Starting Hand Position

Hold the damper pedal
down throughout the piece.

Gliding swiftly ($\quad$ = 86-92)

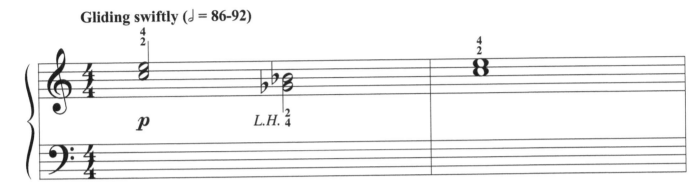

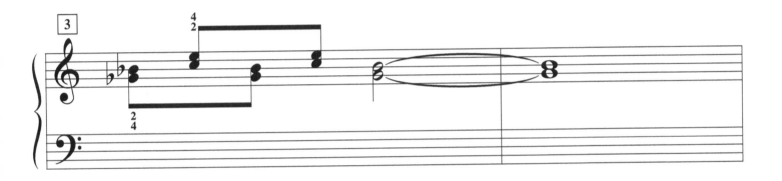

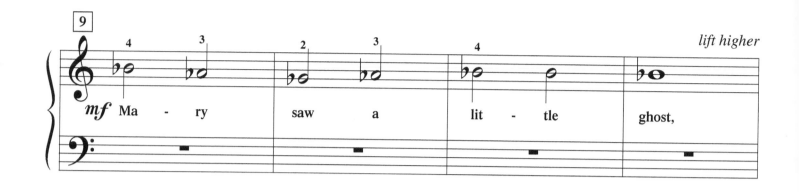

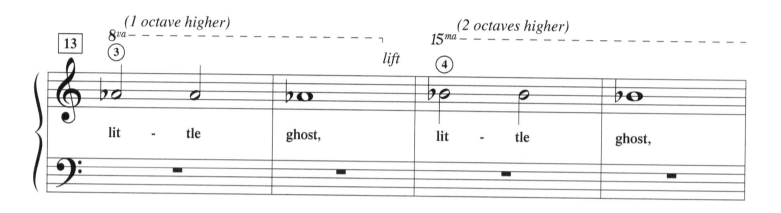

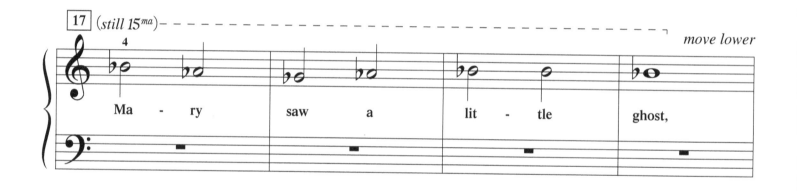

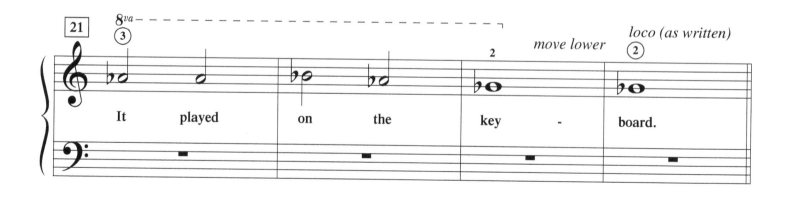

FF1604

DISCOVERY

What familiar song does the little ghost play at the recital?

Concert Sonatina

1. Allegro

Nancy Faber

FF1604

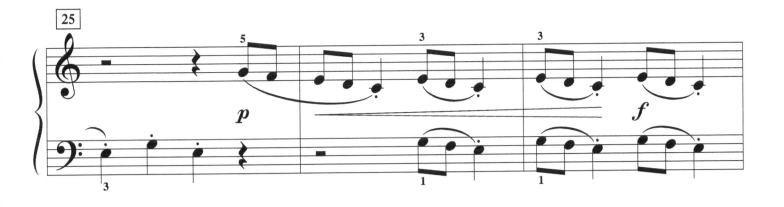

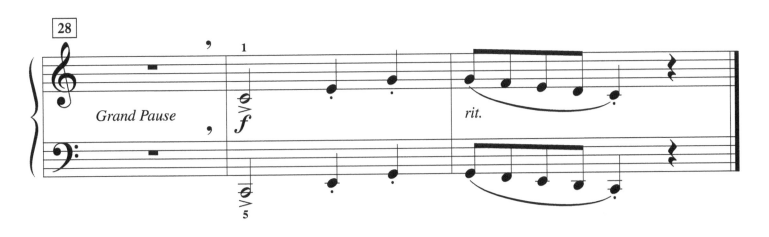

DISCOVERY Name the **broken chord** that begins the piece.
Name the **5-finger scale** that ends the piece.

2. Andante

(R.H. moves to Treble C)

FF1604

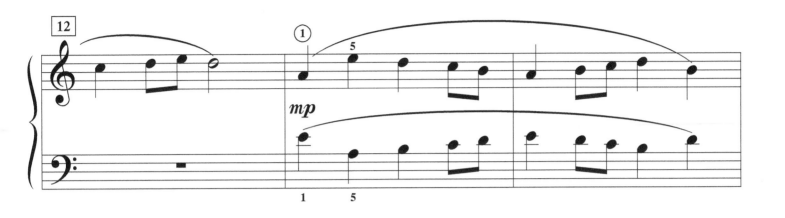

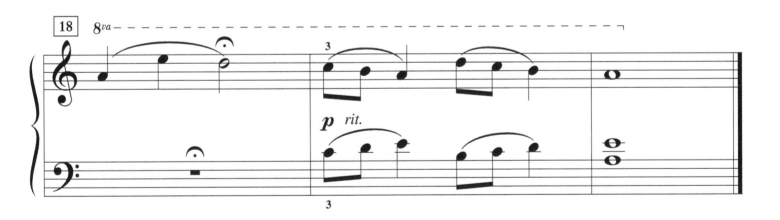

DISCOVERY

Does this movement use **parallel** or **contrary motion**?

3. Presto

Name the **L.H. interval** used in each measure for *measures 1–16.*

Morning Has Broken
Secondo

Play as written.

Traditional
Arranged by Nancy Faber

Gently moving

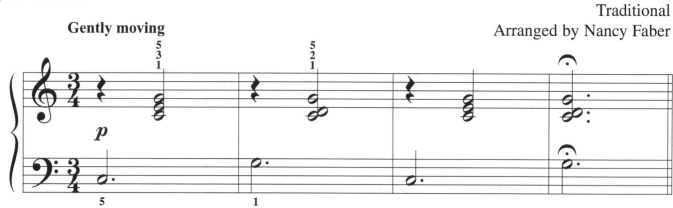

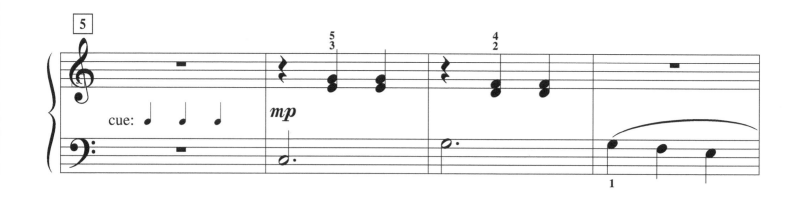

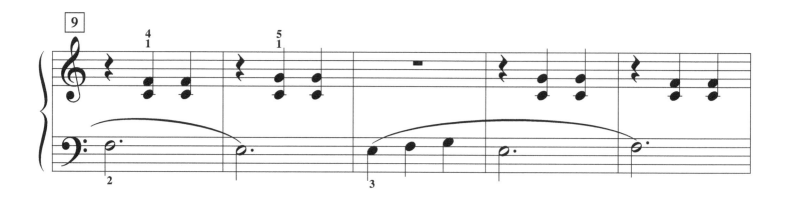

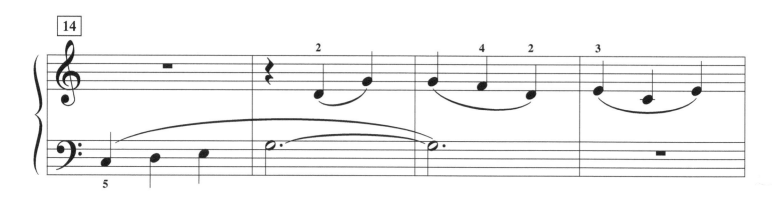

FF1604

Morning Has Broken
Primo

Play BOTH HANDS
8va **throughout the piece.**

Traditional
Arranged by Nancy Faber

Secondo

D I S C O V E R Y On the **closed keyboard lid,** tap the *secondo* rhythm on page 20 with your teacher.
Use both hands and count aloud.

FF1604

Primo

On the **closed keyboard lid,** tap the *primo* rhythm on page 21 with your teacher.
Use both hands and count aloud.

Snappin' Harriet

Words and Music
by Nancy Faber

Lively swing (long-short pattern for 8th notes)

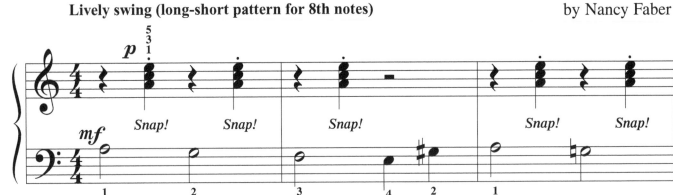

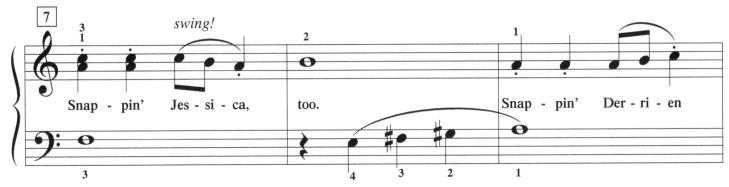

Teacher Duet: (Student plays as written)

FF1604

feels the beat, Snap - pin' An - tho - ny, too._____

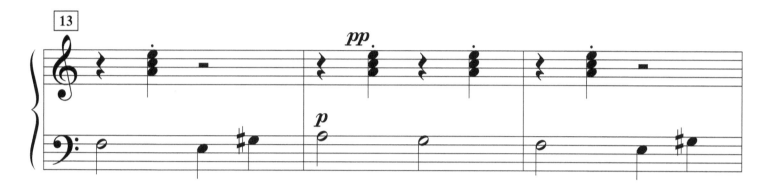

Snap - pin' Chris - to - pher, Snap - pin' Viv - i - an,

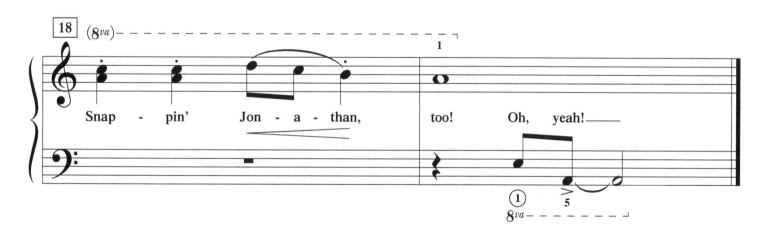

Snap - pin' Jon - a - than, too! Oh, yeah!_____

DISCOVERY The R.H. for this piece is based on what **5-finger scale**?
Can you play an **A minor 5-finger scale** up and down using *swing* rhythm?

Hunters' Chorus

Carl Maria von Weber
(1786–1826, Germany)
arranged

Allegro moderato

26

FF1604

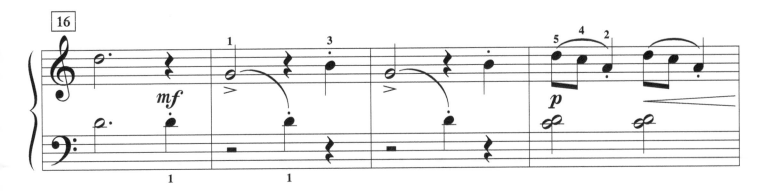

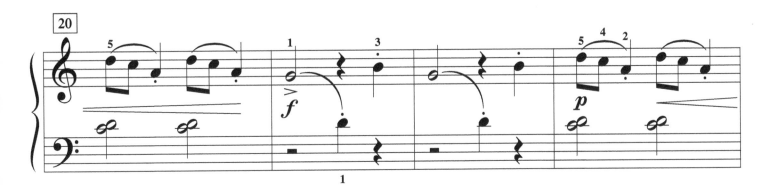

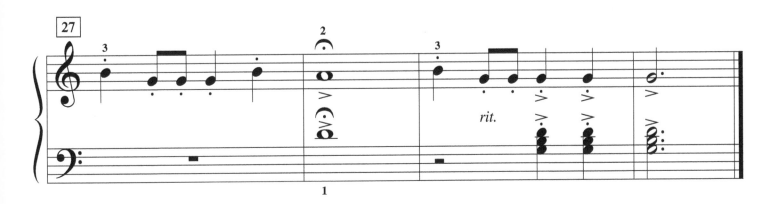

DISCOVERY Find the following in your music: I chord, ascending (going up) **G 5-finger scale**, dominant note, *crescendo*, broken G chord, *fermata*.

Home Run Harry

Words by Crystal Bowman
Music by Nancy Faber

FF1604

(move quickly) ③

a tempo

DISCOVERY

Name the **minor 5-finger scale** used to open the piece.

Teacher Note: Teach by rote using patterns of skips and steps.

 pianoadventures.com/gold2A

First Snowflake of Winter

**Hold the damper pedal
down throughout the piece.**

Nancy Faber

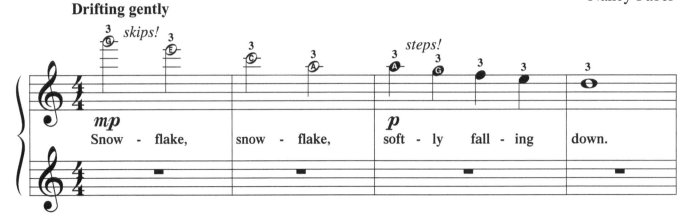

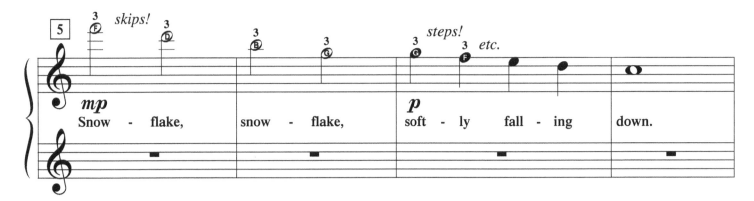

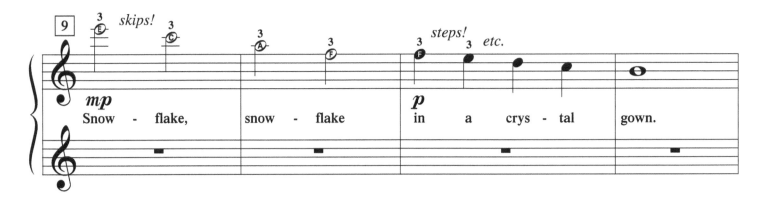

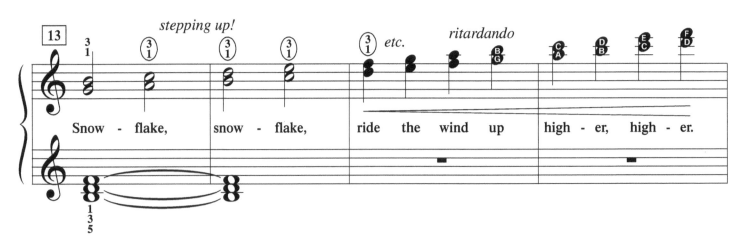

FF1604

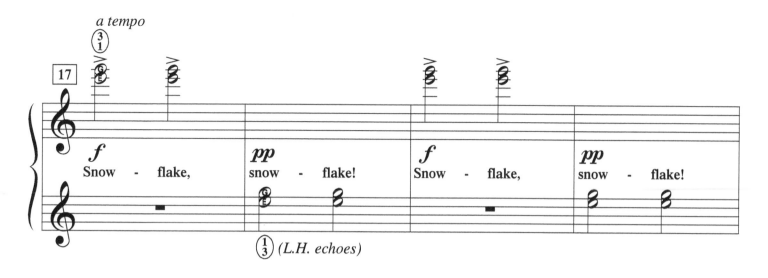

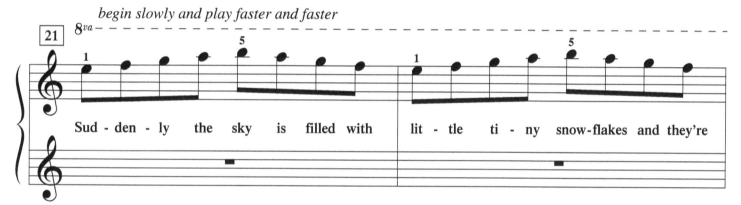

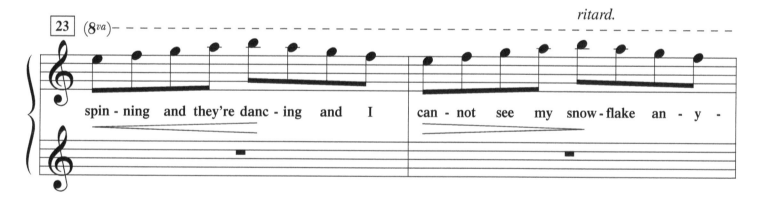

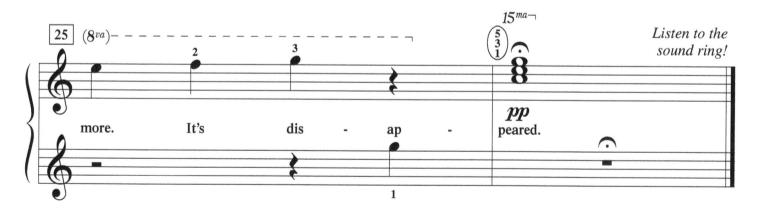

 Musical patterns are used throughout this piece. Your teacher will help you see them. Can you memorize this piece thinking in "patterns"?

Toy Town

Words by Crystal Bowman
Music by Nancy Faber

FF1604

DISCOVERY

What is a **pick-up** note? Why does the last measure have only 2 beats?

FF160

Grandpa Leprechaun

Words and Music
by Randall and Nancy Faber

FF1604

Let's go catch a lep - re - chaun to - geth - er.

If you have a pen - ny, we could try! Lep - re - chauns are

just a lit - tle greed - y; we could find his pot of gold! *Clink!*

move lower quickly

DISCOVERY Where does the melody change
from **D minor** to **D major**?

Gold Star Dictionary

Circle a gold star when you can pronounce each term and tell your teacher what it means!

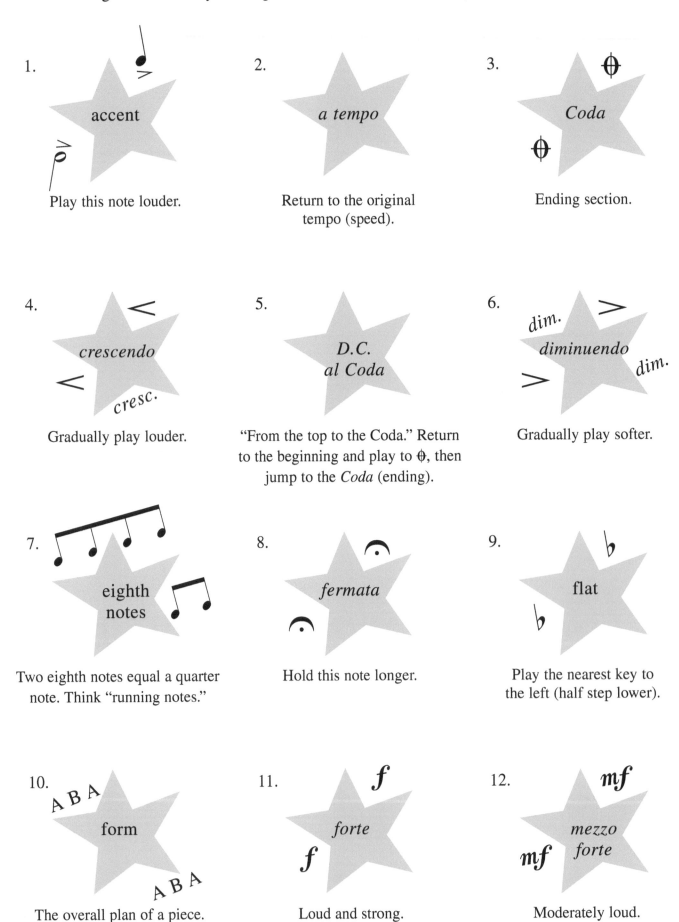

1. **accent**

Play this note louder.

2. *a tempo*

Return to the original tempo (speed).

3. *Coda*

Ending section.

4. *crescendo* *cresc.*

Gradually play louder.

5. *D.C. al Coda*

"From the top to the Coda." Return to the beginning and play to ⊕, then jump to the *Coda* (ending).

6. *dim. diminuendo dim.*

Gradually play softer.

7. **eighth notes**

Two eighth notes equal a quarter note. Think "running notes."

8. *fermata*

Hold this note longer.

9. *flat*

Play the nearest key to the left (half step lower).

10. **form** A B A

The overall plan of a piece.

11. *forte* **f**

Loud and strong.

12. *mezzo forte* **mf**

Moderately loud.

FF16

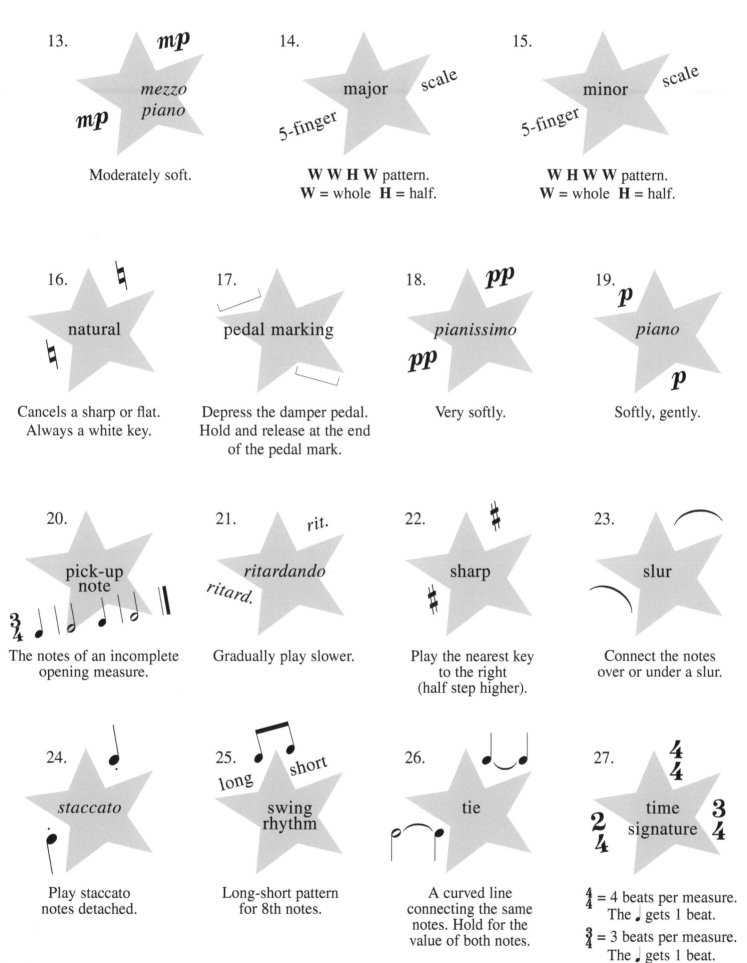

13. **mp** *mezzo piano* **mp**

Moderately soft.

14. major scale 5-finger

W W H W pattern.
W = whole **H** = half.

15. minor scale 5-finger

W H W W pattern.
W = whole **H** = half.

16. natural

Cancels a sharp or flat.
Always a white key.

17. pedal marking

Depress the damper pedal.
Hold and release at the end
of the pedal mark.

18. **pp** *pianissimo* **pp**

Very softly.

19. **p** *piano* **p**

Softly, gently.

20. pick-up note

The notes of an incomplete
opening measure.

21. rit. *ritardando* ritard.

Gradually play slower.

22. sharp

Play the nearest key
to the right
(half step higher).

23. slur

Connect the notes
over or under a slur.

24. *staccato*

Play staccato
notes detached.

25. long short swing rhythm

Long-short pattern
for 8th notes.

26. tie

A curved line
connecting the same
notes. Hold for the
value of both notes.

27. time signature

4/4 = 4 beats per measure.
The ♩ gets 1 beat.

3/4 = 3 beats per measure.
The ♩ gets 1 beat.

GOLD STAR CERTIFICATE

CONGRATULATIONS,
Gold Star Performer!

You have completed the Piano Adventures
Gold Star Performance, Level 2A.

You are now ready to begin
Gold Star Performance, Level 2B.

Write your name in the star to celebrate your progress!